Rake

poems

Shannon Tate Jonas

GARDEN OAK PRESS
Rainbow, California

Garden Oak Press
1953 Huffstatler St., Suite A
Rainbow, CA 92028
760 728-2088
gardenoakpress.com
gardenoakpress@gmail.com

First published by Garden Oak Press on September 15, 2020

ISBN-13: 978-1-7323753-9-0

Library of Congress Control Number: 2020939126

Printed in the United States of America

The human body is the best picture of the human soul.

—LUDWIG WITTGENSTEIN

This is this.

—ROBERT DE NIRO
as Michael Vronsky
in *The Deer Hunter*

Contents

The Ceremony 3

I. The Forest Torso **5**

The Dream of the Green Cave 7
The Forest Torso 8
The Rake 10
Epistemology 11
The Equation 12
The Derelict Orchard 13

II. The First Word You Think When You Wake **15**

The First Word You Think When You Wake 16
The Common Good 17
Spleen & Ideal 18
I Wish We Could Have Been Children Together for a Little While 19
Two Ladders in One Field 20
The Anniversary 22

III. The Underground Film **23**

The Town's Cathedral 24
Talking Shop 26
The Vicinity 27
Both Sons Married 28
The Underground Film 30
The Hauk 32
The Witness 33

IV. The Student's Keep **35**

The Correlation 37
The Posh Geometry 38
The Brothers of the House of Desideratum 39
The Summers I Mowed the High School Grounds 40
The Origin 41
Ennui Within the Son 42
Love Child 43
The Time Spent at the Shore 44
The Student's Keep 45
Two Tragedies of the Leaves 46
To One Who Understood Life More Fully 47

V. Stone Stacker 49

Self Immolation 51
The Fourth Dimension 52
My Sweetheart the Drunk 53
This Mud Fails 54
Appalachia 55
New River Gorge Bridge 56
The Other 57
Hackneyed 58
Michigan Weather 59
Hobo Signs & Symbols 60
Fatalism 66

VI. The Return 67

All I Wanted 69
The Return 70
The Route Between Mountains 72
The Provincial Man 73
Drafting a Will 74
The Grave 75
The River 76
The Dream of How You Undress 78
In the Vineyard of the Self-Righteous 79
The Sword 80

VII. The Gifted Moored 83

The Spider Wedding 85
Architecture 86
The Gifted Moored 87
Vernal 88
That Which Guards the Borders in My Mind 89
The Gray Fox 90
The Hallway with the Wooden Floor 91
A World of Something 92
Watching Birds in Winter 93

Notes 94

About the Poet 95

Gratitude 96

Acknowledgments 97

Credits 97

To the memories of

GORDON DANNY JONAS

&

GORDON TATE JONAS,

fathers both to me.

The Rake

poems

Shannon Tate Jonas

The Ceremony

There once was a breeze you felt across your face
in a field you walked through as a child, where,
simply because you could, you counted the steps
it took to go from one end to the other. The only
thing in the world that could touch a yellow hair
on your head was that breeze that day.

I was ordained so that I could travel
to a place that no horse
could survive by swimming from the mainland to. Me
& my bags & my wine were brought to the island
by a diesel ferry. From the center of my bones I wished
the couple well. I wished their gathered families well,
  as well.
It was quite a sight to see, they later said.

After I performed the ceremony, I skipped
flat rocks across the surface of Lake Huron
& saw storm clouds approaching the shore. It rained
during most of the night, steady & cold.
When I walked through the streets of the island, I felt
somehow out of place,
  hunted peripherally by some surreal.

The island's beds groaned. The house's beds groaned
along the walls. Having acquired an ignominious shadow,
the next morning I left the island & returned
  to where the stars
littered the attic above our bed
  like a neighbor's pulled weeds.
There was a valley we descended to raise a buried fire
to pride & piddle about the many living & dead things.

ONE:

The Forest Torso

The Dream of the Green Cave

Blood falls through his body
like a pocketful of keys tossed
into the middle of the sea.

Having dreamt last night of entering
the green cave to hurl his grandfather's
psalms & keys into the cave's deepest

wells, the sound of the keys, as he
shook them in the cave's face,
served to vivify the cave's holiness.

Blood falls through his body
like a stream of tiny black flies
that pour from the dead tree

with a lightning strike scar that runs
the trunk's length. He thinks of
lightning which requires its converse
to be fully seen, requires an absence of light.

The Forest Torso

Echo ping of struck iron through the forest
during the early afternoon, around one or so,
iron against iron, echo ping that rouses many
birds from investigations, each into the other,
echo ping that clears the heads of many
other axmen, already their boots waterlogged
& thudding through the miles of underbrush.
We never cease in our search for water.
The search for water is continuous & familiar.
Something glows, & we approach it because it shines
before us, like a sound, but it is not a sound,
yet we behave toward it as if it is as it glows,
& in drifts the scent of newly cut grass from a valley
or so away to the west & we remember our chores
& our love of what it is to be here, to be something
alone & outside of what surrounds us, the outside
which we've always known & realized is our
inside, the outside & inside the same, the inside
& outside the same, & we are a part & wish
for nothing more than to be a part & of a whole.
The echo ping awakens us, it is a gleam
of sound that lightens us from our senses,
for we need to be lightened, we cannot remain
so heavy in our skins, these bodies that leave
& move off to be somewhere where we are not,
us, I mean, whatever that is to you,
but you know what it is, when you try to know.
There is an echo ping that disperses through the air
& through the trees with their birds, & another
that remains & glows & we love this emanation,
this giving away & giving off of self which is selfless,
in deed & in body. That is what we know.
What I cannot know you will tell me later
when we are separated by our bodies & minds,
but you will try & I will try & the forest will slowly
live & die between itself & us. That is the body
of the forest, what can be held, apprehended.
I can see you within the body. The lilt of light
on the bed sheet & your body, but not the search for water.

I can drape a flag over the forest in my mind, as a thumb
pressed hard against the earth, & it will drape
its way into the folds of the earth, as this bed sheet
touches your hips & shoulders as light plays through
its own light, gently & with its own physics like a mind,
which is a cloud passing through a cloud, it becomes
itself as it becomes the other, becomes nothing & something.
So the sound glows, issues forth, & now we are not alone.
Like the cloud that has vanished into itself, the next
minute will soon be invisible to us as we devise
its unmaking. The first custom I learned was the accent
of my people who taught me to speak with a furrowed
tongue. They unloaded words from a wheelbarrow

at my shoes, sound after sound, echo after echo,
high commodity within the forests & hills.
The words I learned unmade me as I unmake you
when I speak to you about my first thought that might
have been my one only good thought but I don't know
what my first thought was, only what it might have been,
or when you read the sky & learn about trouble,
that is when you know you might be on to something.
I was visiting the town of my birth the other day,

& looking at a circle of stones in a yard I thought,
this means something to someone.
For I saw an intended pattern, a language.
The dust from my ropes fills the forest air when I
shake them out. The notes of dust are constellations
that now share one dimension when they settle
on the surface of the bowl of water. I drape dusty
rope around trees that will be cut the way
the bed sheet drapes your body, or the flag drapes
over the canopy, the thumb pressed against the earth,
language threaded through my mind, the scent of water.
I see your body, draped by the bed sheet in the afternoon light.
Like a circle of stones, you are. You have to be.

The Rake

A forest must be burning somewhere nearby.
Birds have been flying into the windows
of the house all day, snapping their necks,
stopping their hearts. I made a shallow
pile of their bodies under the bedroom

window. This is the only place I know
when lilacs emerge in February, when
winter should still be young. I think
of a boy old enough to remember
fire who pointed at a flower to describe

what he once saw. I've heard, somewhere,
that what the boy did was poetry.
All day birds have been killing themselves,
flying into the windows of the house.
Their bodies are many. The dirt is pandemonic.

Epistemology

I don't know what is in that tree.
Gargoyles are clapping their hands at
the tree's base, aping their ideas of

what is human. I cannot see you anymore.
In my memory, however, you are a stone.
I can calculate you like a sum of two numbers.

Day & night. Stone & stone.
You were good at life, though I can't
see you anymore. You owe me sleep.

I don't know what is in that tree.
Perhaps you would know what is human
& what is animal there.

Like an oak leaf between the pages of a book
I think of you between the hours of my sleep.

The Equation

Separated from my people,

I watch a motley yellowish leaf
float down the river before
me. I see the trail it makes
in the water.
Tethered to its trail

I make it my aim to study
the leaf daily.

A string of minuscule flies floats
out lazily from the thin neck
of the bottle of wine I open.

The flies settle & sink like dust
midair
into the black water
of my glass.

Their oils etch into
the history of my body.

The bottle has "Live" etched
into its side.

Beyond the bottom of my glass
is the sky at night.

There is a series of crow caws

& they foretell what is to be expected
on the thousands of nights

separated from my people.

The Derelict Orchard

The mountains had been hidden behind mist all morning.
My son as an old man had spent his time walking through
the abandoned orchard, the orchard also covered by fog.
My son was considering carefully
    the last words we shared, when he was
a much younger man,
    words which ended with me saying,
[I will take your word]. He took a smooth stone
    out of his pocket
& held it, weighed it in his hand, felt it in his palm,
    considered
for a moment leaving it as an offering
    in the nook of a blackened
knotted apple tree & then re-pocketed it.
    He continued to walk
through the trees & promised himself one of many final
resolutions to replace any obvious or implied darkness
    with light,
either in writing or in thought. He also considered
the existence of shades & if he encountered a shade
within a far corner of the orchard what he might say.
Many of us decide when it is time to cease to change
as the others change around us. So it is then the others
cease to change within us. Often the cessation of change
arrives after too many wrong sounds
    as we forget our songs,
the songs we invent & the songs we have been given.
My son thought about emptying the shades into the earth
to cleanse them of their wholeness of light. The old man
considered his last words to his father as he felt again
for the smooth stone in his pocket.
    [When you are a young man,
return to this apple grove & there you may find me,
waiting, nearly asleep under a tree, for your heart
to re-inhabit you]. The man left the stone inside a tree,
considered the weather & returned to where he dwelt.

TWO:

The First Word You Think When You Wake

The First Word You Think When You Wake

Open a window, I think.
The light outside is not as terrible

as the light inside this space.
Fasten this to this,

& this will become the outcome of that.
He who walks among walks amongst

the eleventh day of the eleventh month
the eleventh breath of the eleventh thought.

When you mend yourself against
your will when you sleep, every name

you ever spoke aloud returns to the sea
of its birth, whatever idea it is

most at home with, it returns to it.
As the birds dream in their eaves,

the name you think when you wake
is the word for when two crows

call to each other through snow in November.

The Common Good

There is no key to unlock
the door to the room
of the universe dedicated

to domestic failings
though I understand it
would be the size & shape

of a bayonet or machete
& smell like a wet crow depending
on the hand turning the lock.

But this is not about nightmares
of leaving the houses' back stoop
alone in the dark.

I leave behind the machete
when I approach the garden
that serves the neighborhood.

It thrives with fruit & birdsong
that many throats spirit away.
When I watch in the trees at night

those that steal the crops, I free them
only to listen to the morning's song.
In the meantime I speak
of things I remember kindly
like the smell of oil paintings
& blue mountains.

Spleen & Ideal

We leave the shade of the forest
for the warmth & light of the field
that is broad & loud with insects.

There is one tree in the middle of the field.
It has been dead for a long time, you say.
Just look at the trunk. It has been alone

for a long time. We leave the open field,
skirt over the fence, & take our time
walking back over the ground

we have covered. We leave the forest
to walk the field to re-enter the forest
on the other side hunting for shade.

The trees feel like a city. We like this even more
once we address the change. Perhaps we don't
feel so alone, since the trunks resemble an avenue.

We are again among the trees & shade. You say a child
would save my life, & nothing more. I believe that,
though I question your use of the word more.

I tell you I dreamt last night of a boy that
threw scalpels at me for nothing.
I think of my father's mother, who, thinking
of many futures, sewed a dozen quilts
& stowed them into cedar trunks, & her
husband who lives inside my luggage to this day.

Feeling a breakthrough in understanding, I once
recorded my ancestors' stories & speech on tape,
now still unable to withstand their sounds.

I Wish We Could Have Been Children Together for a Little While

Going in fear of narrative lyrics
& lyrical narratives, the night fears
a kind face to talk to & I do. Really
all I wanted was to walk alone very late
at night listening for whatever music
was not my own out there. For nothing
seminal did I search & going in fear
of the rhymes of the past, I love it's

not hard to be with all these sleeping
crows about. I refuse to address
the you. With all these sleeping crows
about I submit to what I lack – we'll
lose all we can lose, that's obvious &
tired as going in fear of anything, it's
tired. May I sleep somewhere awash
in your girlhood's flashlight, my shadow

benignly haunting your hayloft?
I can explain it this way,
un-beautifully: I heeded guesses
for years & years across many states
with some assistance & alone & this
is where I was led, no song to sleep
inside of, enough wounds to share.
The birds offered a solitude for the human.
But the human offered no solitude for the birds.
You sleep in the well of sleep. And
I sleep less well in the coffered, what,
un-song of the night? Beautiful comma, shape
of half my wakeful brain, oblong
scythe – Ah my Evening, all I wanted was
to consider your tongue precisely & know it
before I felt it change like a predictable breeze.

Two Ladders in One Field

I am sitting atop a 12-foot A-frame ladder
in a field, the closest thing here to a tree.

With a mirror the size of my palm
I communicate with myself as a younger man

who also sits atop an A-frame ladder with a small
mirror of his own. Usually he appears very far away.

We both fear lightning. Some mornings
it appears his ladder has moved closer.

Like me, he sometimes sleeps beneath
his ladder. With my mirror, I tell him

I want to be buried in Virginia.
He mirrors back that he wants

to be buried in California. I mirror
back that I understand him clearly.

And that he is wrong. But I understand.
He does not forgive me but I forgive him.

I feel almost like I am his father because
he hates me & blames me for his being.

When he mirrors these feelings I have
no response. I put my mirror in my pocket.

He tends to mirror back angrily when I do so.
Oftentimes I hear a distant lone banjo player

wandering through some unseen gradient of the field
& anxiously mirror to my younger self.

I want him to hear the sound of the music but
he never hears it with me, no matter how close

his ladder. I think we might be able to share
this sound but apparently he either cannot

or pretends not to hear anything of what
I am hearing. When I am especially lonely & cold,

I mirror him to ask if he remembers the New River.
He mirrors about a train wreck but nothing more.

Yesterday he mirrored [The sun above is not
a light. It touches me but I cannot touch it].

I mirrored back he must listen to the music
when he feels alone & cold. He responded

that I myself was no sustenance, [please how
do I get out & stay out, when does the final wine arrive?].

Wishing not to drown in the silver mirrors of the dead,
I mark how often the crows caw above me.
    In the last hour

I have notched seventy-two scores in the top ladder rung
for every crow's caw. [If only I could pull my ladder

into the air from here] he mirrors. I mirror the light
across to myself:
    [When you get there tell me how you are].

The Anniversary

You look down the road
& don't remember the car
that doesn't come.
You still don't remember.

Birds scatter.
Naked field.
Dead skin.
Shed feathers.
Less weight to manage.

Something about corrupted cells,
Last Days & terrifying dreams
though what can be recollected
cannot be terrifying.
Nonetheless, you say.
You still don't remember.

Even though that's not what I said
you say, you still don't.

Something about wild fire,
a horse named Spook & white eyes,
dead milk, if milk can be dead.

You are in the field, you are in the field,
as I was there.

THREE:

The Underground Film

The Town's Cathedral

The summer the lake on top of the mountain
dried up completely & forever, I left
the place of my birth. Then I left the mountain
altogether after having been the last to stay,
finally giving up any hope for the lake to return.

I have since rented a one room hovel on Main Street
in a nearly abandoned & forgotten mill town.
I have learned in pieces of hearsay
that my father spent his boyhood near here,
that his father was a preacher in a small church close by.

These facts are merely chance as I feel little connection.
At times I find myself at zero.
I sing myself hoarse in the dark.
I notice I am stared at when I walk through town.
I think many more words than I say or sing.

We create what we want as we want it to be.

The town & its dwindling people have been erecting
a gray stoned cathedral for over three hundred years
since the town's founding.
I walk past the unfinished cathedral daily, eat my fruit
on the shaded limestone slabs in its yard
as if they were tables hewn for centuries
for a single day's gathering.
I have come again to zero

after I awoke in a large empty aerie atop a smokestack
within the closed paper mill's fenced campus.
I wrote 'You have earned your shade' with my forefinger
into the grease & dust on a remaining pane of glass
after I climbed down the smokestack's side.
As I descended the ladder,
    I imagined I was being watched
by a child who stood on a distant mountain, who sensed
he was observing something miraculous & impossible
    in the distance
in the town of the eternally built cathedral.

To him I was a bird that had changed into a man
overnight & now, unable to fly, slowly & clumsily
was making his way down from the sky
to join humanity as humanity diminished.

The man outside of town thinks that I'm foolish
but he still pays me anyway as always to toil in his fields.

I rotate piles of rocks from field to field,
one rock at a time, with a wooden barrow
that the man's mule drags through the ruts.

This seems meaningful work for me to complete while the
cathedral is being finished.

Talking Shop

The silent isolated farms
are covered by a sea of haze
from a wildfire somewhere
to the west of town.

The smoke fills the world
the way the heiligenschein
of the woman who lived
in this house before me

inhabits my liver. I could sit
in the mechanic's shop & listen
to the passerby's stories
of hotwired boats & squandered

family fortune for hours
but the evening draws out
vulgar language from the calendar
peddler in the corner who knew

my father. Walking home I see
diseased faces wheezing
in the branches. On the porch
a spider lets herself down

from the eaves. She falls
like an ember in the dark
from the celibate woman
ranger's watchtower.

People say after the farms
the town will be next to go.
I open the windows & mind
the whispers & breathing I hear outside.

The Vicinity

Everything here – especially the birds –
does not change. A solitary bee hovers
around the unlit light bulb in February.
Some birds peter about, blatantly alive.

How birds sleep is an absolute mystery to me.
I wish them life but solitarily they
exist beyond me, in a language that
is their own, & so mine is ugly.

Despite the song's beauty, I am left with the
nothing between the notes. That is the thought
of flight from here, a field of corn, now empty.

Both Sons Married

Now is the time to notice the rain
beyond a simple shoulder shrug
once the winter yawns

before an over-mined anthracitic language
that disturbs my sleep –
so I look forward to hearing my wife's bathwater.

Intent is the problem of reflection.
That one intends to reflect is a problem.
Dreams are closer to stumbling along railroad

trestles in the middle of the night
as a very young man infatuated with promise
& memory. Thank god

my soul is not on fire as it was then.
I high-five a bum on the street who is excited
about calendars of Swedish women which were

popular in the mid-1980s. He loathes London
but is somewhat talkative about Paris.
When I ask him about his own country

he wretches & asks if I can swim.
I think of a water beneath our feet.
I say yes, I can swim very well, & he goes along
intent on his footfalls
as if walking across a train trestle, each step
carefully chosen. I call after him,
"Antioch Jurisprudence, wait!"

& he flips me the bird. He blows his nose
& coughs into my advanced degrees.
Whether his name is Antioch Jurisprudence or not

is a somewhat silly consideration. I will sleep
the best I can, despite Antioch & his gesture, despite,
small comfort, the train in the town that carves a deep gulf

into my sleeplessness & the last dreams of mice
gorged on blue poison beneath our floors.
I am at once & the sun is tomorrow's wind.

This is the day. I can imagine the ceremony.
That was the day. The itinerary,
names exchanged. *Something* takes place.

Handshakes. Inane comments on the refreshments
& recent weather. What you want. What I want.
The somewhat literal soundtrack for that day:

Rain. Rain. Rain. Rain. Rain. Rain. Rain.

The Underground Film

We've been filming underground
for weeks. Like God, I've gone south.

Down here in these tunnels & walls
there is seldom any wind,

but it is down here, when I feel
a breeze brush across me,

inside the whole sound of the wind,
I hear people screaming.

Today, by accident, we interrupted
another movie being made.

I opened the door to a stone room
& two women in clear shower caps

were bathing in a porcelain tub, &
by candlelight, filmed one another.

I closed the door, & backed
away out into the echoing hall

having wished them luck with
their film. A breeze touched my face

at the closing of the door. Color
underground is not redolent,

but fragrant. I'm rarely in a grove.
Days ago we filmed a frantic painter

devising a mural with burnt cork
on a wide stone wall in a large chamber.

The chamber smelled of coffee,
though we could locate none.

Leaving the chamber, I pushed against
the door. There was something on

the other side, pushing back.
This is why, before we began filming, I set

a chair in my yard beneath the magnolia tree
to wait for whatever it is on the other side.

The chair is red & made of wood.

The Hauk

It is the 23rd of June
& I am practically swimming in
birdsong. But my eyes are dark.
I went looking for the dead dog.

Placidly swimming in birdsong,
I live for a few days at a time
on an island during the summer.
But today I am in town

& my eyes are dark.
Moi oiyyes are dowark.
Our friends are out of town & so
I am looking for their dead dog.
I do not find him.

The dead dog evades me.
He gives me the slip.
I am on a wild goose chase.
But the goose isn't a goose.

The goose is a dog.
I went looking for the dead dog,
& unable to find him,
I returned, washed my eyes,
shoveled sod on the puddles in
the yard that would not shrink.
Just June, & I'm already tired.

If the dead dog turns up, he turns up.
In the meantime, I listen to & watch
the hawk in the tall pine
across the way from me.

I believe I am beginning.
It seems the small flowers shiver
when he rests & when he is watchful, screaming.
So I watch the hawk. I watch the hauk –

The hauk – more true than sunlight.

The Witness

Perched along a ridge overlooking the Little River
there is a wooden deck or balcony built into the side
of the hill & I watch them trudge up to its dim solar lamps
late at night when the sky is clear, through the rough
grass, carrying bottles of wine & sturdy glasses, lights
strapped to their heads that reflect the spider eyes
that I can see from my roost
    in the oldest cedar on this ridge.

They reach their destination, turn off their lights,
probably look up from time to time,
probably listen to the far off movements of the river,
the rhythmic susurrus of insects moving in the field,
murmur to themselves words I cannot hear,
& soon I lose interest & recall the past day.
I'm drawn to the flight of a Cooper's Hawk,

solo song sung in one's mind for years at a time,
unaltered, vast lyric daystar, un-spooled into &
throughout the river's gorge, poured from one well
into another, the song, like a mind & body, composed
of a screed of seemingly random notes, sung
through systems involuntarily,
    slung through voids as stars arc
along their paths.
    Their being on the deck is random enough.

Consciousness is gravity as gravity implies intent.

FOUR:

The Student's Keep

The Correlation

So these are the night's final stars.
So my voice has changed.

There is no lack of music in my youth.
I will count my age by the length of my hair.

Doctors do not lie
but they do.

The shadow is precious because you can see
it. It is not what you wish, but it is.

When we bid goodnight to the night's final stars,
the doctor had what he called a "change of mind."

According to him, the organic
relationship was reversed:

the health of the solar helix hinged on
the health of the boscage on earth.

The Posh Geometry

Firstly, it is everlasting. Set in stone. *A priori.*
Second, though obvious to all, it is put to language
by one consumed by one's own knowledge.
It is music & it is slow & moves slowly into us all,
it surrounds & inhabits.

Two birds bathe in the birdbath
beneath my window today.

Any two set points of demarcation can be paired
by a single line,

One chair in the yard has been pulled from the table
made of gray metal.
My sight is a straight line from my mind to the chair,
emitted & reflected.

I would prefer not to follow
the first word with another word.
But there is a need for words.

Lastly, there is a need for words.
As the hemorrhaged light of the afternoon fills my being,

the birds through the yard are innately demonstrating
a physics unknown to our bodies.

The Brothers of the House of Desideratum

There is an idea that turns on a switch of an idea
in the mind that cannot ever again be turned off.
There are ideas that grow in the mind
as the facts diminish in reality.
Such as the sound of a bird's song.
Or days turned into weeks.
Days unweave images of birds from their songs.
Their glinting eyes & the corresponding sounds
both fade within the skies & trees.

The first made thing I destroyed on purpose
were a boy's eyeglasses I stole. I smashed them
in the woods adjacent to my street,
    with a rock against a rock.

Another might have learned
    that most actions are begun as intended.

As a community we have organized
    to seek the out of tune
stringed instruments amongst us.
    We clamber down each avenue
& corridor, clanging out our racket on old kettles,
    old bottles,
bison skulls, beaten tin, & tambourines.
We play beautiful stringed songs in contrast to our ruckus.

The tuned cellos, violas, & violins
    are tossed off the bank into the lake.
The discordant instruments are collected & burned
    in unison on the longest night of the year.

The Summers I Mowed the High School Grounds

I've smeared my blood on the front door of a stranger.
Anything that means something has layers to its music.
Those who are quiet enough know this.
The tractor turned over as I was mowing
the hill above the football practice field.
I taught myself how to mimic birds
I admired during the summers. The birds follow
the tractor. They swallow the insects
the blades toss up. This behavior makes me love the birds.
Later, strangers pretend that they visit the capital city
where I've moved on to. I let them believe, almost happily so.
They ask me the progress of certain civic projects there.
I project the news for them & they listen as one.
The woods sound within & the birds never vanish.

The Origin

I traced & re-traced
the history of the skull
& the history is this:
the origin speaks!
He would often look at
& think of his hands where
any warmth was welcome.
He would begin
a new thought before ending
a prior thought when speaking
for he'd thought so long,
his mind was one thought,
long, unending, but not
limitless, without a beginning,
but with an end he could
not see or foresee, or seek.
Often that which appears
asymmetric in nature is really
most symmetric, like his mind
& his hands. For what he searched,
after the sound echoed
& died against & within
the bodies of those
that surrounded, was the sound
he knew not to search for,
nor how to search if he knew
the sound itself, so there, within,
like a cullet array within a dense
wood, or an extinct woodpecker's
croak in a swamp fog, the sound
emanated. It, the sound, aboded within
but without him. Within some square
of fallen leaves where once
a gray fox lightly slept, lilted
sound within sound, as an abode,
the sound he did not know existed,
died.

Ennui Within the Son

My son complains there is nothing to do,
  that he is bored to death.
I tell him to study the dictionary.
He ascends to his room upstairs. I don't see him for days.
I begin to worry about his absence & he returns
to tell me something, perhaps what he has learned, I hope.
He says, We are the moral liars,
  of which little is writ of our true selves.
I say, Every single line is connected to every single line.
He says, You invent meaning to suit you. We all do. What
makes the connections real?
I say, What I wanted you to capture
  from the exercise was knowledge.
He asks, So why do you snigger above what you have created?
I leave the question unanswered & step outside into the yard.
I realize my son has more potential than I.
But I wonder if he is too serious
  to ever be content or content others.

Writ is a lovely word.

Love Child

Poets love nature & themselves are love.
Watching an old woman watch a child
climb a tree to fetch an errant balloon
I believed in the theory of always losing
that which can possibly be lost.
At times I believe in underlining
every sentence that contains the word sea
from *Moby Dick,* of making a diagram of each
sentence by drawing lines of similarities
to form a beginning & further chart my understanding.
Do not forget the constellation that is this animal's
guts. Really, the whale as an idea,
is far less than the thing itself. So,
poets love nature & themselves are love.

The Time Spent at the Shore

The sound of the ocean
A wondrous dour stranger

No one will look me in the eye
I rise later & later each day

The sound of sea gulls
Their calls actually comfort me

It's very cold but one wouldn't know it
By gazing at the sea or sun

It feels like I'm a part of a movie
There is no real eye contact

Music from inside does not fit the outside
Just the ocean day & night

I don't sleep enough to be
Can't sleep into anything

The sound of the ocean
Wondrous dour stranger

Not sure what to search for
The superstition of language

The Student's Keep

What made him seminal,
admired & celebrated was his unshakable sadness.

The day I learned how to apply stitches to a gash
was cold.
My toenails tingled & ached inside my woolen socks & boots
as I was on my feet for hours on the clean solid tiles
in the basement that was once also a bomb-shelter.
When I arrived home, alone before my shelves of books,
I mixed the water & blood
that had been congealed on my hands
& under my fingernails into the stone I'd kept
from the creek of my family so that it became darker
& learned the blood from another.
The light years our eyes have absorbed
will expel from us to the edge of belief,
to an orchard, to the wooden chair reclined
beneath the very old tree.

His body had many visitors,
many taken aback & many without speech.

Two Tragedies of the Leaves

One tragedy is how long it has taken me to
know it is only when it is crepuscular & still
that the world scatters when I open the door
to the outside. When songs vanish, I know it.

There is a bronze snake curled inside the heart
of the magnolia tree I walk under after sundown.
There are blue & scarlet birds that sleep inside
the round white blossoms of the tree & rain clouds

move across the deep green leaves that cover
the ground when the wind moves in slowly
from the west through thousands of pine boughs
& open windows on the way to the coast of the Atlantic.

It is there the birds have changed & assumed
the color of the sea. Brown, mottled, light gray,
dark gray, & silver. For hours the songbirds
leave their young to sleep inside the magnolia blossoms.

The second tragedy is when the snake uncurls at dawn.

To One Who Understood Life More Fully

I mixed my blood with a woman's blood in a room
that had dust from countries separated by oceans,
as if the blood & dust were words that existed
within the idea of me prior to my being, words I shared
with her when we were children & strangers.

This happened after we were married. We opened our palms
with a dull serrated steak knife
    that had been my grandparents'.

I was taught early to associate every door with a tiger
as a tiger might be on the other side of every door.

There is an untitled tome inside a cave in the mountains
whose first word is [soul] & whose last word is [unuttered].
I was told this around the fire as a child.

The rain is moving generally over the country.

Somewhere a son prates loudly before a bonfire.

∞ sideways is a straight line with a beginning & an end.

Having now observed three tigers in the general area,
    my people will not visit me.

Once time was all there was though time did not exist.

FIVE:

Stone Stacker

Self Immolation

sleepless

you know sleep will come

trailing your vatic robe & vespers to your midnight desk
love undress after much ink – lay your head down
I won't touch you – tell me how to destroy myself
I almost said I want my last word

to be your name
but I didn't

•

fire opens itself to the dark
  & the land expands

there will be birdsong here & there will be bread
but it will not bring us back for anything

The Fourth Dimension

the universe in the fourth dimension
is comprised of empirical tears –
the universe expands because we breathe

we are all infinitely connected

in the fourth dimension:
with the living, dead, to come –

I do not judge and luckily cannot number the stars
you watch nine crows escape the bare oak –

the crows are stars

the crows are tears

My Sweetheart the Drunk

– the last kid chosen brushes snow off home plate – essential
gesture – the snow begins anew –
    he's been chosen for this & will learn
the moon is a rare bird – it's fog coming through
    the white-pines – it drinks the river dry

though untouched by rain the moon's a part of our nature

– six strings have snapped in Memphis, TN
– the answer to every question is 'Soon'
– sometimes I can read my mind –

what can we do – tell me & I'll do it
    – the wind at twilight blows through the empty factory
prairie town – blows through the open windows
    of the houses – our hate but not redemption
– the camera at odds with the worried eye
    behind the lens – the outcome the inevitable blur
& the subject that was never
the lost gravestone in the lost yellow field hedged
    by the lost split fence is what keeps me
alive – the daily hunt
– we've not touched God but every inch of sky –

leave your window open tonight & think about me

This Mud Fails

the son heals his friends without effort
the father rhymes in his sleep

I am blessed
I don't have to say everything that is alive is holy
I don't have to say I am young
I don't have to say my love

the river glides through the trees
we know what we know

Appalachia

1.

the sky is possessed & onry

reassembled-fire
the mountains are shrinking, dissembled

dying chords, chords dying
semblance – my mountains

fire is the perpetual motion
all depression
all rise all rise all rise
& be seated

voice and after voice
fire is the perpetual motion
sand & throat & sand & throat & sand
is what is fire

what fire is

the fire is awake
the mountains are withered

2.

I wasn't born at the division of the sea
breathing the sea
I didn't know the shore
but the mountains & I know the mountains when I know it's
like being a child with no speech, when I knew Why –
what hurt & what did not

the boy that I was tells me now when I am afraid
I'd follow you to my blood, my death,
the field that would drink my life
& so I am not afraid

New River Gorge Bridge

the scream
like a loosed arrow
bores a tapered zero
above the nacreous rapids –
births an un-fleshed
womb into the air –
the world holds –
then silence closes
around the perfect

The Other

say the mind is a crutch

– a tool for navigation
– an end table

say the imagination is an eye
no: say a hand

fondle a stone and say I've forgotten how to think

kiss the lover's mouth & say you are god to me
say you are a warm smooth stone on my tongue

– say I do not choose you
– I need you – I feel pain most because you exist

Hackneyed

for Michael Heffernan

any day we are given

rotor & raptor –

  machine & bird

•

machine & bird

•

there is a grave
  for every fifteen keys to the sky behind the sky

the keys move into & out of many pockets

•

there are many machines & birds moving

language moves forward & backward
  – it's what a metaphor does –

•

I drove the school bus to a graveyard
  and we all sat there for a while –
  me – the kids & the birds –

aren't we lucky to be here, I asked
o wouldn't you love to know the dead, I asked
each of us quietly thought for a while as we sat there
  in the bus along with the birds & the
sky – evolving –
what the kids wanted to know was do bones poke out
  of the ground here when it rains &
how gears work – I said don't worry about any of that:
  none of that matters –
I didn't say a metaphor is a kind of lie – I said the birds
  are bone & machine – they sing &
revolve

Michigan Weather

black sand –
a tracker
once said
silt –

here was once
underwater –

the ocean re-seeded

& left inland seas
to the north

•

sand as relic:

grain – sea – bone

•

Michigan weather

•

the flock of geese has frozen above
Lake Michigan

I can count them

•

I fall asleep with wet hair –
the wind smells like ice

– two small hands draw fire from the water

Hobo Signs & Symbols

1.

What alms for the living can I offer –
moth-eaten cloth, parcel of salted tongue, or bovine-heart?
A glass eye wrenched from a frozen hand?
I wander the trees for neglected eggs and shed silver
feathers. I have time to barter & bewail.

The birds trill & trill & trill.

2.

And there was the watchman's lantern that ogled form
within the formlessness; & I peddled
my fear piecemeal to God
who resided as starlight that filmed the earth's hollows
with a bluish caul; & the moon was a milky eye
& I was not afraid.

I recall hundreds of wings stirring above the tracks
nearly every dawn.
I do not know what I held closest

to my body:
the breath in my lungs, the breath
held for a moment in my hands.

3.

Most animals die in the dark, in the reeds
beside the road or the gully along the tracks.

Some I find still warm. Most have clouded eyes.
Some simper into hands I cup to hold their voices.

Sometimes in my sleep I touch
the bodies of deer, gaunt horses, hounds,
lithe and repaired, & sound,
come back. When I wake,

I never know what to say:
Sorrow hangs on some like a robe of flesh,
Or,
I dreamt a lie.

4.

Doak knows of two things he owns for sure.
One is a fiddle with 3 strings.
One is a glass eye he found
in a crow's nest.

Sometimes he lays the fiddle at his feet
& says I'm dead tired.

Sometimes he holds the glass eye in front of his face,
& it stares back at him, unblinking,
like a tulip bulb, like light.

5.

I miss the house where the river sang me to sleep. The house ranged in shades and sound like a season will. There were birds in the evenings & small houses along the road. One evening two women were at work in a garden. They were piling limestone rocks, pulled & clawed from the dirt. They worked at the bottom of a small hill. There were scattered limestone markers at the hill's top. I did not sigh in the unkempt cemetery that wandered the hill like rain. I did not read the names carved into the stones. The trees were resolute in their calm as sparrows doted on the bark's infestations. The two women did not look up from their work as I passed them. I believe they were loading wagons to be carted to a barge that made downstream toward a mansion.

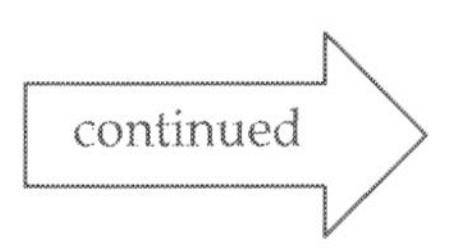

6.

The November night is drinking rough wine
with the mansion-scribes. I'm peering
around the grounds.
Ghosts of great birds lacerate the sky
over a small body of water, a hand reaches for a cello
bow & the furnace grates its fires, lumbering
against the cold.

Along with the wine-stains and fennel there is a severed finger.
It has been on the chopping block since dawn.
The husband is locked in his study.
A servant mills about the woodpile,
fumbling with the logs.

Someone weeps from the reeds by the river.

7.

How the fallen leaves seem to wince in response
to the breath of the coming night: their last exhalation
before the change in their blood, before their salient wither
& our ruminations on fire, this change of season.
Now is the time when the evening can be called piebald.

Sporadic puddles & outcrops of leaves collect the wind
into their frames; fine sand

Between the teeth is a sign of the mountains' erosion.
Sorrel gatherers covet this silt, this departure
to the mundane as the sky spreads its salt,
abrading the teeth of the sleeping,
turning dreams toward enveloping darkness,

the mounting cumulus where the voices
of those we love and have loved recede,
& I rise & wish I could draw a bath, thirsting.

8.

Doak said the last thoughts of the dying are of heat lightning.
It's their dreams guiding them
through the fields of their youth, he said,
guiding them to their long home.

Their clothes are piled at their feet.
  Their boots tighten and shrink,
  having been licked clean by deer at dawn.

Worms digest their salt
  in labyrinths of crumb.
  He says what the dying see also
  are their memories of trees, & the trees
  stir like hair underwater.

The trees wave so long.

9.

O God, it is I, & I've come to, awake again. The sun is cannon-fire, I once told a man. I saw a glass eye in a dream, a star hovering within the brush, & I was drawn to its light, & I approached it, tipping no leaf, like a ghost. The eye was shining. It was Doak's voice. I've learned some dreams are common. I see myself freezing and thirsting for water, pale-sick & losing teeth, the river's creosote & slag, the water orange & slow, when each breath is a prayer, & I know that I'll not last long. I saw a man draw tight the load in the bed of his truck. I thought that he would step out of his shirt the way Doak stepped out of his skin when he froze alone on the river-bank, fingers taut as fiddle strings. Men from town thought he had drowned. They trolled the river & from a barge sounded the bottom with cannon-fire. His body did not raise. The birds were missing.

continued

10.

The storm has passed. Leave it to the trees to bear
the silvered frost, to bear the varicose canopy,
night of a thousand fingerprints.

The sky's damp linen is caught
on November's half-sunken nails.

Something shared: hunger's bond. I rest in the twilight
under the dim sun that has drawn copious blood.

11.

A human-light singed the leaves.

An afternoon storm waylaid the rising dust.
The 13-year cicadas
have emerged in their buried-skin. Vespertine branches
swallowed the thrushes,
the red sun, the swallow's hunt on the wing.

There is grief in me because
of a departure I cannot hold in my hands.
In the shade the wind uncovers remnants of a resting body
in the dust. What's left behind are scattered vacancies :
the eyes of statues that would follow one
through an empty house. All eyes of men
are colorless in dreams, essentially devoid.

In dreams we do not age.

The breeze rustles the fallen leaves,
the cicada skeletons, to & fro.

12.

Always the river at midnight. Silver-eyed fish circle the moon,
cradled in the sunken johnboat; its dim likeness films
the water's surface.

The trees are without song. Doak, birds watch as you wade
beyond your waist. You've shed your body.

It grows frost on the bank, quilted
slowly by copper leaves.

13.

The sun lies shattered beneath the pines. It is a light that goes out in my mouth. The shade twitches across Doak's eyelids, a visible breeze. We wait for our socks to dry. Silence is our voice repairing & this choice for quiet separates us from birds. Last night, a new moon & incessant song from the trees. The song was a place I walked, a branch under a branch under a branch. I imagined a sustained warmth in my mouth after a third cup of tea, closing a book, listening to the darkness through the pane. Birdsong has taught me listening is a form of prayer & want, taught me to bow to the troubling dreams brought by the song that simply is, the song that is to the moon that is not there.

14.

I carry a light with me to bed. I tell Doak
I'm watching for his ghost.

I sleep. I dream. My mouth opens. Enter what will.

15.

Tonight I have two questions for the fire:

> Why does all light leave me un-nourished?
>
> What in this world can heal us?

Fatalism

when we turn off the lights in this house

what is left in the absence of light

is a wandering

& decimated tribe of gods –

& now the anodynic kneel when I wash my face alone
 – the coward's hour –

you lie asleep like a body of water I wish I had discovered
a mirror that holds my form –

nine crows yonder rouse & spread outward –
away from us –

the sky clears

SIX:

The Return

All I Wanted

I've not seen anyone set foot in this field for a week
The new wet hay smells like spilt whiskey
If you're looking for someone you're not meant to find her

I've not seen anyone walk down my road for a month
I forwarded a decade of mail on to the Mid-west
Where the wind passes through with no beginning & no end

The Return

I have decided to give all of my land to visitors & strangers
after I woke in the night, my sight a ghost limb.

On this day all the crows in the yard will vault
into everything but the all of sadness when I leave.

I have recently been invited by mail to a commemoration
regarding the town of my family's birth,
    soon to be covered by a narrow deep lake.

I thought that I might try to go back –

The action itself more important
    than any setting I could describe.

But to return –

The torn bird wing I found beneath the hedge in town
    looked like a taught shrunken harp.

I counted the stones in the foundation's masonry
& in the handmade bridge over the green creek.

There were too many stones to tell.
There were three thousand thirty-three stones exactly.

As a child the coldest stone on Earth found me, the stone
that has locked my hand & heart. Take the stone. Rid me of it.

Or I will bury it in the lake's water so no child can find it.
The stone from my hand could drift down to the lake's bottom.
Then, was it ever even here?

Someone should heave a gravestone with the town's name
    into the heart of the lake.

Whose name it was that was on my mind as the sun descended
behind the mountains will not go to the grave with me.

I remember the brown blood on the red door. I can't
go back, but I may return.
Whose door it was I never knew
    but I wanted to leave my blood
alongside it as an echo, my own life's arc,

my own life, an echo, a ping.

There was one thing I kept before the valley became a lake.
It was not the pump where I washed crow hearts
    under cold water
in the yard. But the pan that held the water.

The hands in the graves now beneath the water become water.
There are fish that must wander
    through rooms in moored houses.

My father decided to join me to mark the occasion.

Into light into which I could never ascend,
    my father floated upine
on the surface of the lake, hovering above the town of his birth.

As a child I pretended to drown in the bathwater
& danced in a circle outside the tub, reborn.

The Route Between Mountains

I have been straddling the apex of the house
that was under construction for weeks during the day
& sometimes at night. The house is now untended,
unmaintained, derelict, packed with snow.
In time, a common country hovel.
The home of a lone owl.

I dream the owl offers me his frozen eye
& I swallow it. It is then that I see,
looking down from the pines on one ridge,
the cars wind through the valley, switching
on bright lights to avoid the deer & vermin.

Under the sky & weather, the day changes.
We are mostly instructed what to say by custom.
The day is gray, graying. Only small things move.

The mold spreads room to room
through the phone lines, through our speech,
into the walls. I live in a warehouse
in town but visit the house nearly daily.

In the warehouse I count
more coughs than birds.

It is a clear day & I straddle the apex of the house.
There is a large bird calling, croaking,
moving from one ridge to the other,
above & across the frozen river, fields, & valley,
above me & I watch his shadow fly
across the stubble field below & before me.

I will leave the warehouse & live in this half-made house
with its simple walls, floors, & no plumbing.
I will become the revenant of this house.
I will watch over it & stare at the visitors outside
standing in the drive, peering through the windows.

The Provincial Man

In three days my wife will leave me
who I nearly left myself when she was
aroused by a balding neighbor man
in the valley so I said to her stay, then,
if he is what you want & she said "an axe
will come to it." I know not to try to pry the axe
from the hands of a woman in Virginia
as an axe in a woman's hands is one
of the final mysteries of any lifetime.
The final axe is always hers.

Yesterday she said, handing me wine,
"There's great depth in that. It will bring a serious
man to greater seriousness. Will bring
him his eight Decembers, make him
forget to wake on Mondays, forget
the purpose of his razor, & every warning
sign he's ever learned."

In three days my wife will leave me
& the ones that hunt for me will be the pastors
who live mostly for future losses.

Drafting a Will

Death the end of knowing
is smoking in the breeze-way
with your 5th Grade teacher
as you play kick-ball in the multi-purpose room
Death is in his basement tonight
drafting hours of rain for the Atlantic
& playing a drum-set made of wood
from the Methuselah Tree
He drums to the music in his headphones
You know that tonight there will be no sleep
what with death drumming in your basement
& that you will die soon
leaving debts & bottles of cologne to your widow
& mute son who only stares at your face
& cries

Death went back in time & invented
the plantation He poisoned all the wells
in his county & defended himself in court
He spoke any language the jury asked him to
The jury asked him to channel Jack the Ripper
He wilted to the floor & under the table
He spoke in tongues
He was acquitted & carved his initials
into the foundation of my widow's house

Death went back in time & invented baseball
He plucks out his own eyes every night
& rolls them around his mouth with his tongue
As if they were thawed grapes He swallows them whole
& pisses visions & dreams into lakes & rivers that fall as rain
over oceans & fields & cities

Death has never touched himself
never studied his hands

The Grave

The cemeteries are full
& I am always thirsty.
What I want most on Sundays,
I'm never privy to.
Flowers could not be any more un-ceremonious.
Your fingerprint you left
on my face, washed away,
now expanding
in an ocean –
Of all things, only life is reciprocal.
Yet even the dog knows we're dying.
What can you do for me?
What can I do for you?

The River

There is a kind of near-dream that arrives
& announces its presence
when I am at rest recalling
sight of the strange fields surrounding
the river at night, in the form of a scant scent
of lilacs from the bedroom,
in a cheap glass vase with gray water,
losing a dozen petals an afternoon,
while you are out in waders,
since just after dawn in a creek
trying to find whatever it is that drew
you there seemingly without question,
despite having never waded a creek
alone in your life, I believe
the river & dewed field you've
crossed to get where you are have
something in them akin to dreams,
though, here, where I am,
all I hear is the river falling into
itself & the rocks below my
steps gurgling their slow histories
about bare foot crossings & blood
let by buried & rusted coffee cans
& the silt that once here was disturbed
by falling bodies, a man & a tree,
years & years apart, one for gravity,
& the other for love, but for whatever
body that falls, I am aware of mine
for now, as I hold it in my senses,
as my concentration on the water-sounds
is broken finally & inevitably by
the continuous barks from an unseen
far off dog or maybe hound that enters into what I
may deem is my mind but what is, if nothing
else, something outside of myself,
which is momentarily simply the sound itself,

which echoes off the surface of the moving water
& off of the surrounding rock cliffs
& into the rocks below the water
that I pull out from the bottom & drop
just to see how they drift into the current
& settle with a blooming cloud of silt
I think I understand fully as I float
downstream, absorbing the somehow
intent yet random songs
that originate from the overhanging limbs
as the current carries my body.

Eventually I leave the river.

I hold onto my inner tube
& scan the strange terrain before me.

I walk slowly home
to the house I barely know.
The rooms change color again.
Out from beneath the dining room table
there is an empty chair pulled to face
the front door. The room changes color
again. I lay on top of the sheets
on the bed in the bedroom.
I layer my chronicle of dirt on the sheets.
I hear a dog bark somewhere
outside. The barking dog makes me think of a cliff
above the river I drifted past once –

the flowers drop their petals.
The room again changes color.

The Dream of How You Undress

I dream of how you undress
your body in our bedroom
the day before I die,
on the day I die,
& the day after I die,
as if one day were connected
with another.
The images of each day
are practically the same.
You shed your clothes,
you lay your body across our bed.
You could not be more beautiful.
You listen to the sounds around you –
the ceiling fan whir above,
cars passing on the streets,
an anxious dog in a nearby yard, maybe,
& you release your breath out into the world.
We once shared the scent of honey-suckles near the river.

In the Vineyard of the Self-Righteous

Even that what you do is right & your fingers still bleed,
bless the weeds about you & your consoled bones.
We have done many things to be where we aren't anymore,
but none so small a thing as describe to those who need
it most what is an original culture. A faint knell?

The wind blows the topsoil so we turn our backs against it
as we stumble through the exposed roots of trees & vines.
I wish we were more alone than we are, together.
But there is a shape to this, this small hill on which we stand
& meander atop. An unseen dog barks, maybe vicious for love.

It seems the wind & hill welcome your life
& even your shadow is precious.

The Sword

– I have yet to spend the proper time.
I have not spent the proper time.
The time, properly.

– Your face is becoming white at the edges.

– Because it is rotting away.

– Your face evinces squalor of the spirit.

– Because it is rotting away.
Because it is improper.
Because it is my true self.
And, there is a vicious rate.

– You mean there is a vicious toll.

– No, rate.
Of improper time,
of time improperly,
of improper spending.

– We sleep beneath our separate sheets.
Is that some sort of lesson, some punishment?

– For time spent improperly.
Or my face rotting away?

– For your squalor of spirit,
in a dark room, sitting,
& listening to the low,
far off approaching thunder,
& the sound of another,
breathing in sleep,
in the dark, listening,
sitting, in a chair, the far
off thunder, & another,
breathing, in sleep,
sitting, in a chair,
your squalor of spirit, sitting.

– At what rate? My spirit rates in squalor?

– I wish to know why you sit, in a chair,
& listen, to another, breathing
in sleep, at times free from your spirit,
free from squalor.

– At any rate, a round seed falls
into the water
below the overhanging tree.
The water shrinks & expands
the way organs digest organs
that digested organs that digested organs.
Each case resembles how the
eye works. Or the mind.

– Would you call this
The Illusion of Dimension?

– There is no proper time to say this,
but I believe I should so I will.
This is the last drop of rain.
The last drop.
It runs. Runs down this leaf.
Drops into the ground
& mixes with the dirt.
It does not help make wine.
It does not make more rain.
It does not create anything.
No thing.

– So the last drop of rain is squalid.
Like your spirit, like your face.

– Like my spirit,
like my face.

SEVEN:

The Gifted Moored

The Spider Wedding

The spiders in my mirrors have copulated.
I saw your body fall through the clouds
below me. The night was quiet & I should have
heard. All I could hear was the wind through
the pines & the mouse that lives beneath
our bed. The mouse sounds like two pine
boards moved against one another.
When I rose from bed last night,
the house was still. I thought about
the lamb with no thought about the wolf.
The cricket in the night's throat holds the doctorate
of eschatology. The wandering viceroy in the night
with his churlish & diminutive script ogles
darkness through darkness. I feel sorry
for the wind that must touch his face &
I feel sorry for sleep that knows everything
there is to know. I saw your body fall through
the clouds below me. Through darkness
into darkness I touch your face.
I wed the spiders, each to each, just after dawn
on the twelfth of the month.
I performed the service in the room of the house
with the window into which the sun sets.
Cast into ether, the spiders soon took possession
of every mirror in the house, their webs like
filament in a light bulb, causing the mirrors to shine
when the lights in a room were turned on. Spent
of any fortune, I have left the house to them.
All that remains inside the house are the mirrors
inhabited by the spiders, who spin wigs for ghosts
who pantomime comedies as clowns, flawlessly
convincing in their representations of colors.
I have left them to themselves.

Architecture

To know what it sounds like
I lay in the other room to hear
the music playing in the room
I once was in. I've been in
thousands of rooms or so
for seconds & days & years
& all are different & I've changed
few if any of them. You were
with me in a few of them, as I recall.
History describes the vile. Art, the beautiful.
At times. When I reach for you, I'm trying
to be that. Like you I've been in thousands
of spaces. Like you,
I remain in only a few
& am with you there.

The Gifted Moored

Eventually the house's roof began to leak when it rained
so much so that the upper story was uninhabitable.
I thought of the entire roof floating away through
the streets, of straddling the crowning, sharing
my few loaves of bread & belongings with the gathered
crows. Relentless rains carried me down through
the mountains. I felt spruce limbs brush my sleeves
during the night as I passed through the valley
& I drank rain water that I wrung from my socks.
The night passed like a progression of deep chords
that emanated dully from the waterlogged rafters.
I thought of myself as piloting a church through
the riven waters, my congregation of crows
sniggering into their wings at my gesticulations
caused by the storm as I cursed the thunder.

It was early morning & the roof of the house
moored to a pile of boulders at the valley's bottom.
I squinted into my surroundings, the sun
streaming through the trees that remained rooted.

Three things crawled one by one from the attic
to join me on the roof. My crows had fled &
I could hear them croak from the trees,
commenting on the scene at their feet.
The three things made no sound but one pointed
what had to have been a finger to my forehead.
There was a woman's voice in my mind.

I wished to be unmade into my beginning.
They were further silent for a few more moments
then opened the window into themselves & crawled
back inside, unavailed to the gift, or unwilling to give.

Vernal

Evacuating its home of insect
hulls & onion-skin wings

the spider scuttles from lung to lung
inside the black bird's body-cavity.

A solitary wasp hovers around
an unlit light-bulb in a broken

light hanging unused from the roof
above the library porch in February.

I have the world's wine & will
cross seas to read & to write.

I wished this as a lime-green
snake balanced on a limb

in the magnolia tree. The snake's eyes
reflected the sun. Later, I shone

a flashlight onto the face
of the moon. So I sought.

I waited until just after dusk.
Having sought, I walked

into my backyard among the many pines
& cast my vote.

That Which Guards the Borders in My Mind

A nacreous though sanctimonious voice
  issues ledgers from the closet & a nacreous thought.

I tried not to describe the small man, gnome really,
crouched inside our fence in the backyard corner,
but here it is, in a long line:

I said to the gnome, "Gnome, I used to wonder
  what you did around here all day & after
  having spent a day with you now I know
  what you *do* do around here. You guard
  the house when we sleep.
  Perhaps you arrange our dreaming."

I thanked him, & good for him, that gnome, looking, not at me, but at the air in between, a pearl of sweat on a Titan's chest, a shark following lethargically the wake of the swimmer in the center of the sea.

For an exercise in ecphrasis, air the blood.

The Gray Fox

The scream of the gray fox woke me before dawn.
The last thing I remember hearing was a peal
of thunder weeks ago. The thunder woke me
that morning. But I was already awake

when the fox screamed. I knew it was a gray
fox because they are the only kind of fox
where I am. There are no reds. And reds don't
scream– they bark. Lurching in & out of sleep,

I knew the gray fox was just outside my window.
I sat up in the low branches of the magnolia
tree the next night, a headlamp banded around
my head, waiting to turn it on into the fox's eyes.

But no fox appeared under where I sat. I heard
a distant train moving through the city, the first
songbirds rousing. I licked my month-old scab & hung
my headlamp on the hall hook. In the house in the red chair I
sat down.

The Hallway with the Wooden Floor

I married an artist who hated to paint.
We painted together once
well into the night.
When I laid down later, from the attic
a new skeleton descended into my body.
It inhabits me now, somewhat like a soul.
I can see myself, but I have little sense of its
construction beyond my visual sensation of its form.
My body is a drawled sound in the world.
What is there to learn anymore
but what others think?

The lesson is, I never intended to paint seriously
but did so anyway. The lesson is
I cannot teach myself a lesson.
I cannot define the term lesson.
I cannot step outside of myself.

My skeleton is now fixed, captured, fixated.
My fist can become the sun
or block out the sun.
Like words I tell you.
Like your body can become,
on this side of life, where we house
our audible voices.

The sun sank & it rose.
& the window framed your shape
& you left the window.

& you left the room. The house.

A World of Something

When the soul of Albion, the light frigate *Oblation*,
sailed back into the Northern Hemisphere, I noticed
the village was rife with cardinals.

Ruddy cardinals & scarlet cardinals were twining
the air, in & out with their wings & eyes.
It was a village of song & red. Then

the light frigate *Oblation* caught its course north
through the Strait of Reluctant Yawps. The
mountains turned blue under their awnings.

The apogee of air was rife with cardinal song.
I was standing somewhere in the middle
of the village & I heard what surrounded me.

In this world of something, the elder topiaries
in the village caught the lightening from a
town over. Those fires stood outside me

as the gate to the irises closed. Then the air caught song,
& met with the green sea, the air whose skin was
as taught as the wind between the blown sand.

Watching Birds in Winter

Birds fall like water from the trees
emerging through the mist of the gray
morning-time to hop about the floor
of the forest. Something behind my ears
sounds constant & high pitched, like
a machine on the horizon. I see you
drop your shirt after walking home
in the rain. It is as if I wasn't there,
though I know what I saw. I see you
drop your shirt on the floor. You have
been walking in the rain. It is as if I am
not with you. As if I was born
in a separate century. But I see it.
But your shirt still falls.

NOTES

My Sweetheart the Drunk: The poem's title is taken from Jeff Buckley's posthumously released and unfinished album, *Sketches for My Sweetheart the Drunk.*

Hobo Signs & Symbols: The poem's title refers to the cryptic "Hobo Code" or "Hoboglyphs" used by drifters in the early 20th Century through the Great Depression.

The "Code" was a system of symbols used to inform travelers of opportunities or dangers that might lie ahead or about an area in general. Often these symbols were found depicted on fences, walls, and buildings. These drawing were particularly helpful for conveying information, considering many of those reading them were likely illiterate.

About the Poet

Shannon Tate Jonas is the author of one chapbook and a full-length collection, *Battle Sleep,* winner of the Brick Road Poetry Press Prize.

He received his PhD from Western Michigan University.

His poems have appeared in *Barrow Street, Cider Press Review, CutBank, DIAGRAM, Hotel Amerika, The Iowa Review, Mississippi Review, San Diego Poetry Annual, Tammy, Third Coast,* and *Typo.*

His work has been translated and published in the Dutch journals *De Honingzaag,* and *Kluger Hans.*

He lives in Buffalo, New York.

GRATITUDE

Thank you

to the editors of the journals where versions of these poems have appeared,

to those I know are always there, in Virginia and beyond: the JONAS and DEHART families,

to BILL HARDING at *GARDEN OAK PRESS* for working with me, trusting in my work, and publishing this book,

to ROBT O'SULLIVAN for his tireless support and for including me in the family of poets who reside in San Diego, and

to JEFF WALT, part of this community,

to NANCY EIMERS and WILLIAM OLSEN, for their continued friendship and encouragement.

to my brothers in poetry MATTHEW HENRIKSEN and ADAM CLAY –

to HEROES.

My most thanks, always, to INDIA.

ACKNOWLEDGEMENTS

Some poems in this collection first appeared in these publications:

***Cider Press Review* 18.4**: *The Underground Film*

The Fabulist: *The Dream of the Green Cave*
The River

Rhino: *Hackneyed*

***San Diego Poetry Annual* 2018-19**: *The Forest Torso*
Honorable Mention, **The Steve Kowit Poetry Prize 2018**

Tammy: *Two Ladders in One Field*

***Typo* 5**: untitled sections of *Hobo Signs & Symbols*

***Typo* 22**: *The Town's Cathedral*

***Typo* 28**: *The Spider Wedding*

CREDITS

Cover: *Blue Ridge and Wire*
art by RILEY PRATO

Interior:
illustrations by RILEY PRATO
pages **35** and **49**: photographs by the author

Author:
Cover and *page* **95:** photographs by INDIA JONAS

Manufactured by Amazon.ca
Bolton, ON

28782392R00057